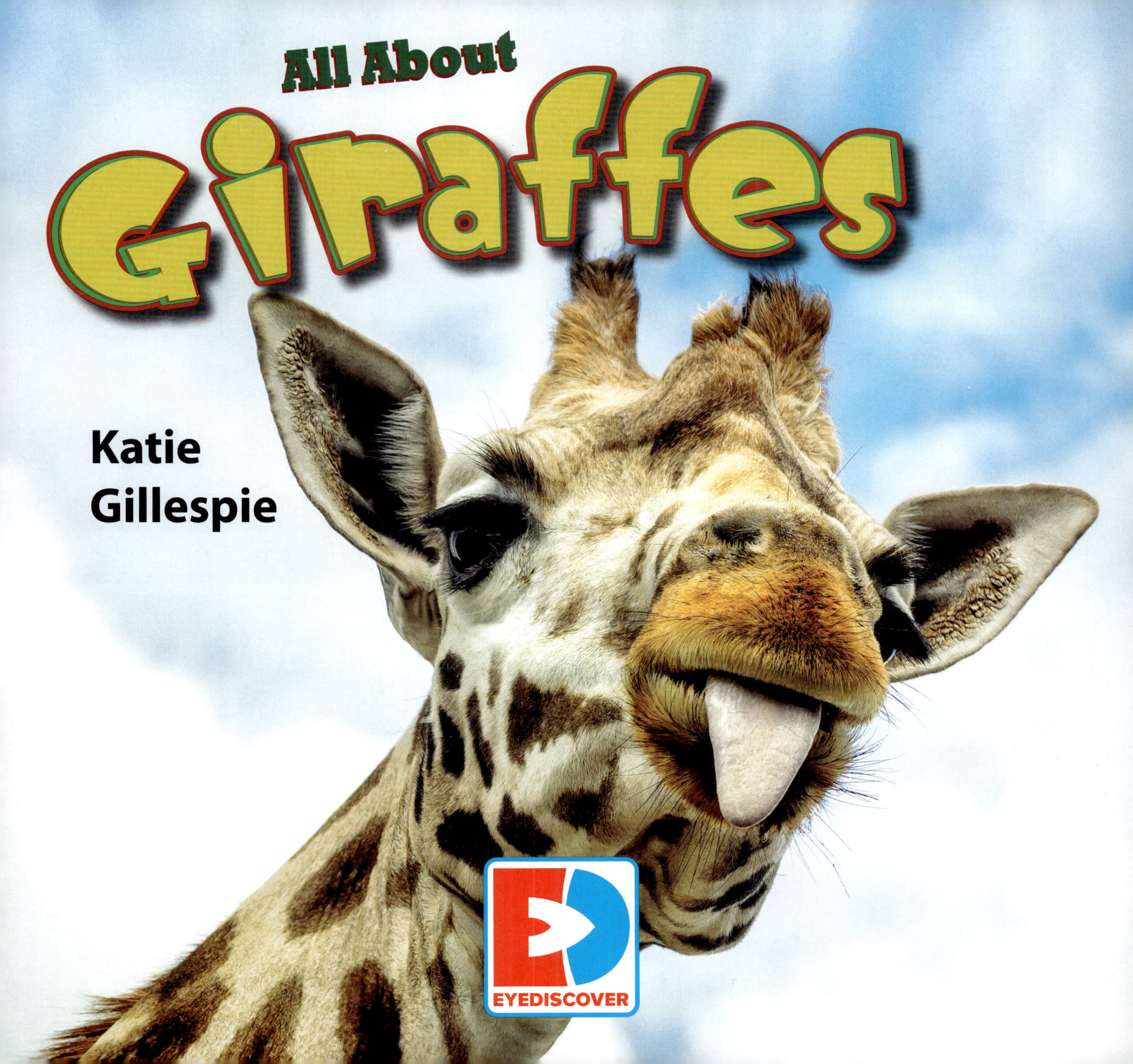
All About
Giraffes
Katie
Gillespie
EYEDISCOVER

Go to www.eyediscover.com and enter this book's unique code.

BOOK CODE

P377999

EYEDISCOVER brings you optic readalongs that support active learning.

Published by AV² by Weigl
350 5th Avenue, 59th Floor New York, NY 10118
Website: www.eyediscover.com

Library of Congress Control Number: 2017930713

ISBN 978-1-4896-5656-8 (hardcover)

Printed in the United States of America
in Brainerd, Minnesota
1 2 3 4 5 6 7 8 9 0 21 20 19 18 17

022017
020317

Editor: Katie Gillespie
Designer: Mandy Christiansen

Weigl acknowledges Getty Images, Alamy, and Shutterstock as the primary image suppliers for this title.

EYEDISCOVER provides enriched content, optimized for tablet use, that supplements and complements this book. EYEDISCOVER books strive to create inspired learning and engage young minds in a total learning experience.

Watch
Video content brings each page to life.

Browse
Thumbnails make navigation simple.

Read
Follow along with text on the screen.

Listen
Hear each page read aloud.

Your EYEDISCOVER Optic Readalongs come alive with...

Audio
Listen to the entire book read aloud.

Video
High resolution videos turn each spread into an optic readalong.

OPTIMIZED FOR

- TABLETS
- WHITEBOARDS

- COMPUTERS

- AND MUCH MORE!

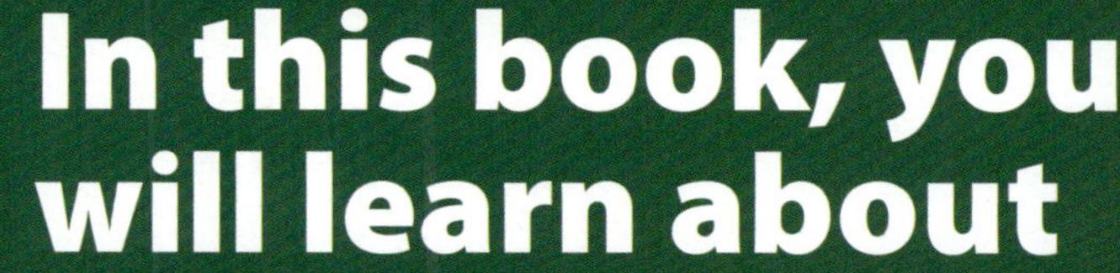

- how they look
- where they live
- what they eat

and much more!

Giraffes are mammals with very long necks. They are the tallest animals that live on land.

Giraffes live in Africa. They make their homes on open plains.

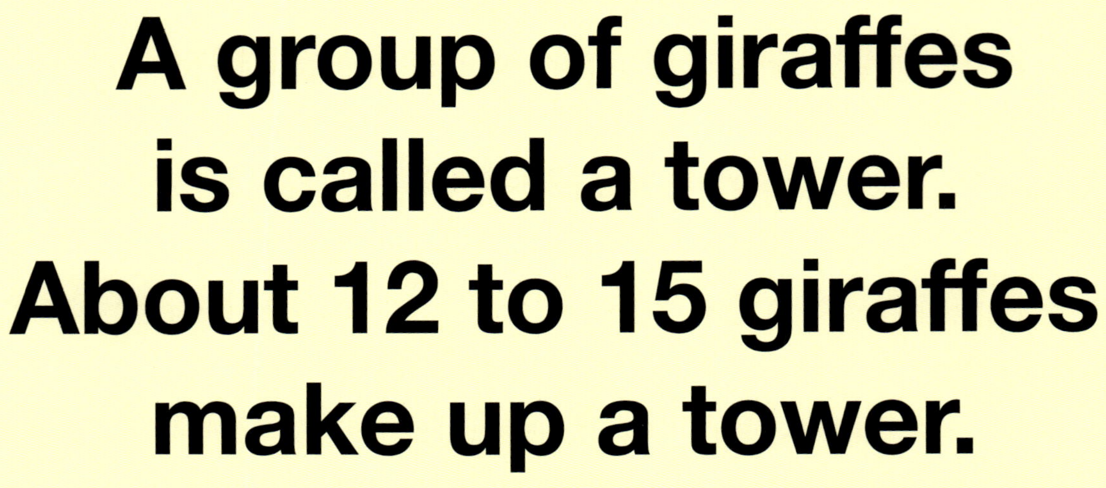

A group of giraffes is called a tower. About 12 to 15 giraffes make up a tower.

10

A giraffe's coat has many brown patches. Each giraffe's pattern is as unique as a human fingerprint.

Giraffes can run very fast. Their legs are taller than most people.

Giraffes eat plants. Leaves and shoots from acacia trees are their favorite foods.

Giraffes have purple tongues. This dark color keeps them from getting sunburned.

Giraffes do not need to drink very often. They get most of their water from the plants they eat.

The number of giraffes left in nature is getting lower. Giraffes need safe places to stay happy and healthy.

GIRAFFES BY THE NUMBERS

Giraffes have only **7 bones** in their **long necks**, just like **people**.

Giraffes **only** need to drink **once every few days.**

Baby giraffes **grow 1 inch every day** for their **first seven days.** (2.5 centimeters)

Giraffes **only sleep** for about **5 to 30 minutes each day.**

A giraffe's **tongue** is more than **1.5 feet long.** (0.5 meters)

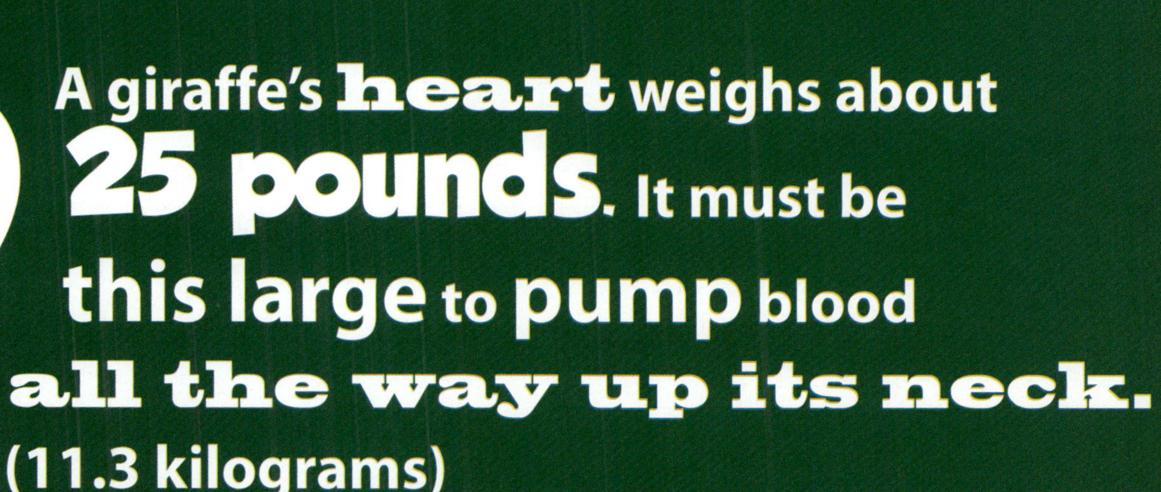

A giraffe's **heart** weighs about **25 pounds.** It must be **this large** to **pump** blood **all the way up its neck.** (11.3 kilograms)

KEY WORDS

Research has shown that as much as 65 percent of all written material published in English is made up of 300 words. These 300 words cannot be taught using pictures or learned by sounding them out. They must be recognized by sight. This book contains 52 common sight words to help young readers improve their reading fluency and comprehension. This book also teaches young readers several important content words, such as proper nouns. These words are paired with pictures to aid in learning and improve understanding.

Page	Sight Words First Appearance
4	animals, are, land, live, long, on, that, the, they, very, with
7	homes, in, make, open, their
8	a, about, group, is, of, to, up
11	as, each, has, many
12	can, most, people, run, than
15	and, eat, foods, from, leaves, plants, trees
16	have, keeps, them, this
19	do, get, need, not, often, water
20	left, number, places

Page	Content Words First Appearance
4	giraffes, mammals, necks
7	Africa, plains
8	tower
11	coat, fingerprint, patches, pattern
12	legs
15	shoots
16	color, tongues
20	nature

Watch
Video content brings each page to life.

Browse
Thumbnails make navigation simple.

Read
Follow along with text on the screen.

Listen
Hear each page read aloud.

Go to www.eyediscover.com and enter this book's unique code.

BOOK CODE

P377999